THE PEACOCK PRINCE

THE PEACOCK PRINCE

(Inspired by the Mahabharata and folk tales)

V BALAKRISHNAN

ZERO DEGREE PUBLISHING

Title: The Peacock Prince
Author's name: V Balakrishnan
Copyright © V Balakrishnan 2021
Published By: Zero Degree Publishing

Zero Degree Publishing
No. 55(7), R Block, 6th Avenue,
Anna Nagar West,
Chennai - 600040
Ph: 9840065000

e mail: zerodegreepublishing@gmail.com
website: www. zerodegreepublishing.com
Printed at Manipal Technologies, India.

First Edition by Zero Degree Publishing: December 2021
ISBN: 978-81-954399-6-6
ZDP Title: 42

Cover Design: Meera Sitaraman
Cover Photo: M Sivanesan
Typeset: Vidhya Velayudham
Printed at Manipal Technologies, India

Dedicated to the truth of those far-back times

The play premiered at Spaces (Chennai) in 2014, and travelled to Ranga Shankara (Bangalore) and the *Soorya Festival* (Palakkad, Trivandrum and Thrissur). The play was also a part of *Theatre Binge* (2017), organised by Chennai Art Theatre.

The initial cast and crew of the play was:

Anuradha Venkataraman: Amba, Shikhandi, Drupada, Sthuna, Bhishma

Vishwa Bharath, Meenakshi Viswanathan: Music

Scene One

(*Amba, the princess of Kashi, stands in front of King Drupada
to demand his help.*)

AMBA:

Drupada, in this world there is no young girl
in a more difficult situation than I.
I have been robbed of friends,
wronged by the person I loved,
rejected by my family, and all because of that
arrogant Kuru dotard - Bhishma.
I was taken away by force along with my sisters.
Robbers and knights fought over me,
killed and screamed eternal glory,
while my flesh was in the pincer grip
of he who had sworn celibacy.

I appealed to the virtue of my kidnapper,
beseeched him to hear me,
"Bhishma, it is against human nature
to force your brother on me.
My sisters seem appeased or worn out,
and happy to decorate the bed for the man
who needed you to show courage on his behalf,
but I love another.
Surely your terrible vow
of never a woman, never a child,
does not shield you from knowing love.
It's what your mother had for your father.
Your brother cannot take me
knowing I am thinking of another.
My lover, he expects me.
Send me.
Permit me to go."

Drupada, to Bhishma's credit,
he did allow me to leave.
Or was it his mother,
who knew unrequited love and its transmissions,
and made love to a stranger in a boat, in the open?
I do not know.
But I was hustled away from their presence.
I reached the house of my lover,
an intelligent man,
but intelligence kowtowed
to gripping fear and egotistical rambling.
He minced no words.

I was a woman desired by another.
How was that my fault?
I was a woman touched by another.
How was that my fault?
And so what if it was my fault?
If he loved me as I loved him,
would he not participate in my life,
in my journey of brambles and thorns
as easily as I had?
I had walked miles to be with him.
Dusty, dirty and unfed.
But all I wanted was to be with him.
And he had issues with who had touched me
and where I had been touched.
He accused me of not having protested amply
while I was being violated
by the mercenary of an impotent king;
of having a cheerful visage,
while I was being molested and taken away.
He said I was ravished by another.
How could he accept one
who had been accepted by another?
I was told to go where I pleased,
and not waste his time anymore.
What was I supposed to do?
Tell him I was weeping
when I was being physically roughed up?
Swear to him
that I was not ravished by another,
that I was a virgin?

Play the wide-eyed lamb
and beg him to take me in his harem?
Drupada, I was choking with humiliation
and bathing my eyes in tears.
Abandoned by my father, my lover, ha! even my kidnapper,
I left as he mocked me to return to my abductor.
I had not approached him for a solution.
I had approached him by my resolution.
And I was in a conundrum.
Who was to blame for my predicament?
I myself, who challenged Bhishma to let me go,
or Bhishma, who had kidnapped me by force?
Or that father of mine
who set up a market for me to choose a husband?
Should I have leapt and run away to my lover?
Then maybe, he would think better of me.
Shame on Bhishma! Shame on my idiotic father,
fixing as the dowry, valour!
For his daughters to be sold at a price.
Shame on myself, shame on that lover of mine!
I was besmirched with misery,
and Bhishma was the cause of my difficulties.

Drupada, with these thoughts I left the city,
and went to the forest
to seek a person who would avenge me
by battle or austerities.
I met devotees who resided in hermitages,
who worshipped the fire and practised hard penance.
They said with ease, "What can we do?"

I begged them to instruct me in austerities,
for I knew that revenge wouldn't flow
without an adamantine body.
They wanted to take me to my father's place.
They wanted to ask my lover to accept me.
They told me to return home and
place my trust in my father to do what was "proper".
They wished me happiness,
for only the father, or the husband,
is supposedly the refuge of a woman.
The husband in smoother times.
And in times of difficulty, the father.

Drupada, I was delicate, not disadvantaged,
for being a woman did not preclude austerities.
I requested them to let me stay,
and learn the secrets of asceticism.
They went to the extent of warning me
that men may covet me
upon seeing me alone in the woods.
Ha ha… even the ascetics in their holy domains
see the single woman as vulnerable prey.
Soon they found me a champion, a man of repute.
Again, I had to retell the story of my humiliation,
revisit my trauma,
and relive my desperation.
I told this champion:
I was of character questioned.
I was not willing to return to my parents.
I was living in many fears,

one of them being disgrace.
The champion misread me, and
said he would coax Bhishma to marry me,
or defeat him in a fair fight.

No no no no no no,
I wanted Bhishma dead, killed, slain.
I was not permitted by my sex, my lineage, my tutelage
to fight him myself.
Bhishma was trained from childhood to kill.
He knew the secrets of war—a war monger.
How could I fight him?
My need was this: To not die without cause,
but to kill him,
to see him die,
to see him violated.
Stripped of his pride and arrogance,
to see the mist of humiliation in his eyes.

So, if he wanted to support me,
then he must kill Bhishma.
I stood there with a flicker of hope
that this champion could
what none else would.

But he saw me.
He saw me as beautiful, as youthful, as delicate,
and wanted to make amends
for what would be lost—youth.
A receptacle for violation.

I was a woman and what course for me to take
but lie on my husband's bed?
How could he decide the form my revenge must take?
Or did he misunderstand my eyes, my visage?
Where I sought death, he was trying to haggle
to make me Bhishma's wife.
That was supposed to be my choice of life.
So, he would ask Bhishma to take me.
If Bhishma refused, then he would defeat him.
How much clearer should I have been?
I wanted Bhishma dead.
Nothing more. Nothing less.

"Please slay Bhishma or I continue in this distress.
Bhishma is mean, covetous, spirited and arrogant.
I have made this resolution.
Bhishma must be slain."

Drupada, the champion, that axe wielder
still refused to read my heart.
He was fixated on seeking a masculine resolution:
To make them listen to him
or beat them into submission.
He wanted peaceful means
as his axe was growing heavy on his frame.

I spoke one last time,
"Kill Bhishma! That is what I want."
The champion asked Bhishma to take me with him.
Bhishma called me a snake

that lives in one house and sighs for another.
Then they fought.
Then they were separated by elders.
Why should two warriors die for such a silly cause?
The cause of a humiliated woman.
They embraced, exchanged pleasantries and gifts,
and went their separate ways.
I was resolved to stay.
Bhishma must die!
Bhishma was warned.
He knew my resolution.
He knew my discontent.
I was spied upon by men,
each act of mine reported back to the doyen.
He was impressed upon
by his friends who could alter destiny,
to negate that woman's tepid curses;
her individual resolution.
They assured him
she would end up a nun
or seduced into submission.

I ventured deep into the forest.
I practised superhuman endurance.
Emaciated, rough-skinned and bronzed,
I lived on leaves and water from the rivers.
I roamed fierce, propelled by my one desire:
The destruction of Bhishma.
I was spat upon by all alike,
they said I was acting crookedly,

my objective, unattainable.
I was weak, a woman.
I was cursed, my monthly menses dried up.

Drupada, I had been undone by Bhishma.
Despoiled of happiness.
I wanted his destruction.
Peace of mind would be mine
only when Bhishma was slain.
My existence was one of continuous misery.
I had been deprived of a husband.
I was neither man nor woman to Bhishma.
I must watch him die.

I went deeper into the forest
where I met strange people
who did not belong to this world,
and there I saw him,
a youth,
a very handsome boy with a spear.

I asked him if he would fight Bhishma for me,
and he gave me this garland instead,
made of indefatigable flowers
that never seem to lose their scent,
and said, he who wears this garland
will cause Bhishma's death.
For all that is born, must die,
and all will be caused by matter.
All matter will be governed by action,

and all action inspired by stimuli.

This garland, he said, must be worn
around the neck of they who challenge Bhishma,
and Bhishma will die.

Drupada, I have wandered the entire earth.
No one dares take this up.
They either hold him in reverence or shake in fear.
His beard by now is white,
and they see that as his piety.

I have heard, Guardian of the Panchala riches,
that you hate him with ample cause.
You are strong and a warrior of renown.
I offer you this garland.
Be Amba's champion, for she is not allowed to fight.
Wear it and kill Bhishma.
I ask you, warrior.
Do this, for I am beseeching you,
like a good woman is supposed to.
That man won't fight me,
or else, I promise you, I have enough fire within
to burn him alive.
Take this garland, Drupada, and kill him.
You will have my eternal gratitude.

Drupada:

I have no need to hide behind words.
Let me spill it without ado.

Bhishma frightens me,
garland or no garland.
I have not the tenacity to approach him.
His spies, you said, are everywhere,
and I am sure he knows
you are here, talking to me.
What will happen next
is not a happy thought.
For my sake,
for that of my kingdom and my family,
I need you to leave.
Yes, it's true I am consumed
by hate towards Bhishma
and I won't stop short of necromancy
to destroy him.
But today, right now,
my loins tighten, my thighs tremble,
at the very mention of that man's name,
Bhishma.
Leave and don't enter Panchala again.

Amba:

More than the disgust I feel frothing perpetually for men,
I am disgusted with this state of mine.
If a man is what I need to be
to kill Bhishma, then so be it.
If it's an appendage between my legs I need
to seek my cause,
if it's a penis that is required
for me to kill Bhishma,

then I will not be dissuaded.
This garland can stay here in Drupada's hall.
Let it remind him of his cowardice and valourless act.
What good was his penis to him?
I will die, burn, and die,
again, and again, till I have the form of a man
to slay Bhishma.
If a woman's victory in battle does not count,
then as a man I will destroy him.
Oh nature, let me recollect every memory of mine,
as I travel from one birth to another,
till I kill that man.
I will enter fire and burn myself,
burning as bright as the wrath in my mind,
for the destruction of Bhishma.

Scene Two

(*Amba has been reborn as the warrior Shikhandi because of a prophecy.*)

Shikhandi:

Let me fight.
Who cares how massive his army is!
I will educate him on who I am.
He who questions my masculinity,
my prowess, and my ability.
I am the first-born of the Panchala king.
I am Shikhandi!
Have they not heard the elders say that
I was born to avenge my father's humiliation
at the hands of the Kurus?
Who remembers or cares what the vendetta was about?

I am a man, and let no one believe otherwise.
I have been ordained in all the rites and rituals.
I wear the clothes of a warrior.
Father, why are you so afraid?
I have excelled in my education,
archery and every other martial accomplishment.

I did not urge anyone to find me a bride.
I am still so young.
You went ahead with stupid astrology,
and yoked me to that girl from the southern country.
Why does that girl call me a woman?
Why does she not see me as her husband?
What makes me a man?
Only an appendage to penetrate her with?
By God, if penetration is what she needs,
I could do it with anything. Even a rolling pin!

No no no,
I am not right in spewing venom at that loving girl.
What will she know but what she was taught to repeat?
How will she know what makes a man and what a woman
when she has been conditioned to see a man
as nothing more than a fool sowing seed?
She was within her rights to scream and shout,
and complain to her relatives.

Now her father marches towards us,
with the intent of killing my father and me,
and delegating his men to rule this country.

What a travesty!
The father was waiting for his daughter to be mounted,
to proclaim his piety and virtue.
I spit upon them all.

This is no deception.
Shikhandi, the only son,
is a man by birth, by his parents' wishes and by his
education.
I will meet that father-in-law of mine,
and slice his appendage,
and then ask him, "Are you now transformed?"

Father is scared, the great Drupada is shit-scared.
Not that he will be killed, but that he will be found out
to have lied to the world that his child is a man.

It was no lie.
He desired a son, to revenge himself against Bhishma.
A prophesy was made
that his child would be both male and female,
decreed by destiny not to be otherwise.
But when, by time made opportune,
my mother conceived me, held me,
and then gave birth to me—
a child of great beauty—
Drupada proclaimed with pride,
his son was born.
Yes, a son indeed.
Now, suddenly he feels I am

not the man he was pinning his hopes on
to fight the Kurus someday?
He stayed so quiet
when the messenger from the king
said I was a woman,
from folly wedded to his daughter
for a handsome dowry.
He did not respond
when the minion threatened war, rape and murder.
He mustered a puny, "It's not so!"

Does my father now suspect me
of not being his son?
Was he ever in doubt?

They have started arrangements to fortify the city.
The priests are lighting blazing fires to please the gods.
Earthly force and godly nature will combine to succeed.
My father and mother have given up on me.
If only they would stand up and proclaim,
"Our son, Shikhandi, is a man.
He needs no penis to prove it."

Your daughter could be penetrated
by a bull or a stag,
yet it would not make men of those animals,
they remain bestial.
I am a man
and they did perform all the rites for me,
for the son I am.

They are scared about the preservation of this city,
of its people and cattle.

Oh father! Sacrifice me!
That is the least of my concerns.
Tell me it's to save your lives and country
that you are giving me up.
Don't call yourself a fool for calling me a son.
You backed my mother when she said I was your son.
Don't call me anything but your son.
Don't hang your head in shame.
I am a man.
I have caused them grief.
They remain afflicted on my account.
I refuse to be dragged before women,
to be stripped, to have the lack of a penis proclaimed,
to hear it proclaimed: I am not a man.
I would rather die.

They can say it was in a fight.
All egos satiated, peace will be reclaimed.
I remember as a child, when I saw naked boys,
I would run to my mother and ask:
"Why is it different between my legs?"
And she said I was superhuman, not common.

But my parents did not deceive me.
I was born a man
and that is a truth
even the creator cannot challenge.

Drona did not protest when I went to him for training.
Why can I not just fight and kill
those who threaten me?
If I were to fight and kill or die,
the truth of my being will still hang upon my father's neck.
My wife will not allow me in her bed.
I would rather die.
This deep and lonely forest lies abandoned,
just as I have abandoned my house and
as my house has abandoned me.

(*Removes clothes and sits in yoga.*)

Scene Three

(*Sthuna sits and starts wiping Shikhandi's body, caressing the limbs, and fanning the air. He has got some food too. Shikhandi breaks the meditation and is startled.*)

STHUNA:

For what purpose do you fast,
meditate and punish yourself?
Tell me your desire, and I will help you fulfil it.

SHIKHANDI:

It cannot be done by you.

STHUNA:

I can surely do it.
I have some well-kept secrets

of alchemy, metallurgy, medicine, and weapons.
What do you pine for?

SHIKHANDI:
Tell me first, am I a man or a woman?

STHUNA:
You tell me first, are you a man or a woman?

SHIKHANDI:
I am a man.

STHUNA:
Then you are a man.

SHIKHANDI:
My family faces destruction.
The lords of the south march
to take possession of all that is ours.
They claim we cheated them;
they have sworn annihilation.
I need to be a man in accordance
with what they seek in a man.
And unless I can exhibit those traits,
I will be a woman, a cheat,
and will be killed.
Their daughter, my dear wife,
saw my body on our wedding night,
and screamed that it was no different from hers.

And hence, I am what she is, a woman.
Silly way to equate things,
a child's resolution.
But I was deemed an anomaly.
And unless I can grow a penis,
and mount her in sex,
her father claims it is a violation of marriage oaths,
and the punishment is death.

My parents are losing their resolution.
The obduracy with which they reared me,
diminishes as they cower in fear of censure
and seek answers in smoke and incense.
I am confused. I want to kill myself.
It seems all will end well
when I end this life!

STHUNA:

You seem to have travelled here from dreams
and carry with you the pain of a multitude of births.
On an average day, I would have walked away,
for crafty as I am,
I don't have the solution to all human resentment.
But I do have a solution for you,
and don't talk of it outside.
It's a simple procedure, an operation of sorts…
of magic and medicine and herbs and skills.
I can transfer my penis, my 'manhood' to you.
And you may flaunt it for a few months.
Once your issues are resolved, your father-in-law sated,

your parents placated, you copulated,
you may return here
and give me back my flesh.

SHIKHANDI:

You seem to be a master of your own will,
roaming the lands and water and skies.
I am so desperate that I will take your word for it.
I will take your sex and
give you mine in return;
and that which is yours, I will be back with it.
Today, I need my city to be saved,
and my parents spared their shame.

STHUNA:

It's complicated.
So, let your trust serve as the pact between us.
Now, eat these herbs and sleep.
When you awake,
keep your loin cloth tight,
and return home with ease.

Scene Four

(Shikhandi is standing before the Panchala court.)

SHIKHANDI:

I am male, dear father-in-law.
A man as manly
as you and all those stuttering fools around you.
Ask them to not flaunt their swords, sheath them well.
I fear they may injure themselves.
What vile conduct do you accuse my father of?
What criminal act do you censure us with,
and seek, without delay, a battle to answer it all?
You have been screaming that you will slay
our ministers, offspring and friends.
What misinformation are you relying on,
which is so unworthy of belief,

that you threaten me, your son-in-law,
and wish to widow your daughter?
If a war is what you want,
then I will give you one.
But not without reason.
If my wife is to be orphaned,
then I must know why.
I am a man, father-in-law.
I don't need anyone to validate it for me.
Yes, my wife has some misgivings.
So let me resolve it with her.
I don't need intervention
in my domestic misunderstandings.
I know what I was born as,
and I know myself to be my parents' son.
You have strange rules etched in stone,
and call upon me to follow them.
I spit on them.
I don't need a beard, moustache,
firm chest and penis
to be a man.
I don't need to be bashful
and breasted and bleed
to be a woman.
I am a man, and if my word is not enough for you,
then I should dismiss you.
But you are my elder,
a father figure,
father to my dear wife,
and I must appease you.

You want me to strip now,
here in front of you and your retinue?
Or would you prefer to test me in private?
I prefer it in public, for it's more revealing
of my nature, and more importantly of yours.
Sure, let your daughter, my wife
have this privilege,
the privilege of humiliating me.
I stand for my country's safety.
So, without hesitation, strip me.

(*The daughter enters and disrobes Shikhandi. As he stands naked, she dresses him again, falls at his feet and leaves.*)

Scene Five

(*Shikhandi, alone.*)

SHIKHANDI:

How this appendage mocks me,
makes a travesty of my masculinity?
I will return it at the soonest, to he, to whom it belongs.
I feel like a fool, challenged for my beliefs,
succumbing to their proclivities,
and becoming a prosthetic man.

There is something strange churning within me.
Was it for my earlier desire to die, commit self-immolation
that I am being haunted by these ominous visions?
I see a woman in front of me.
Who is this woman?

What does she seek in me?
Why is she engaging in austerities
of superhuman endurance?
Fasting, punishing herself, motionless?
Why is she dressed in bridal finery?
Who has wronged her?
What does she want?
She jumps into the flames again and again,
shouting and dying,
for the destruction of Bhishma.
She kills herself again and again.
Who is this woman who stares at me with hungry eyes?
Her eyes locked at my loins,
not lust but pride.
She looks at me like a mother at her child.
She coaxes me to follow her.
Where does she lead me?
Am I going mad?
Why, why am I tired and hallucinating?
Is it the herbs I ate in the forest? Is it a prophecy?
Who are you?
Why do you torment me?
Or is it the after-effects of my surgery?
I see a garland.
Yes, I know this garland.
It hangs on a crooked nail in the main hall.
I remember some story about it.
Some mad woman who cursed father.
I have a desire to wear that garland now.
Why, why… what is happening to me?

Where is that garland?
I want to see it.
I have seen it before.
I want to wear it.
I wanted to earlier as well, but
I was not allowed to.
Now I must. There it is, the garland of the mad woman!
Ah, I feel a stirring in my loins.
This is some masculine perversity.
Why am I in ecstasy?
The borrowed possession is taking hold of me.
It swells and my heart feels its tumescence.
I don't need it to be a man.
The woman screams, "It must be so!"
Rigid, turgid, tumescent revenge.
It rises to remind me of revenge.
Against whom? Who?
"Bhishma", she whispers… it echoes in my ears.
The penis rises and wishes
to proclaim itself as me.
My father was never bereft of a son.
I was bereft of a penis.
Now, I have mixed energies.
Shikhandi the man,
sports the manhood of another.
And she speaks from within me.
The garland unites her with me.
"Shikhandi, arise and fight Bhishma!
He cannot reject you,
as he rejected me, Amba."

"Amba? Who are you?"

"I am you. You are Shikhandi, the man.
I am Amba, the woman.
We are one, not separate.
You are the angst
of my soulful yearning to be a man.
I am the anger
of the woman who was never allowed to be born a man.
Destiny has conjoined today.
The purpose for which you were born
is the cause for which I died:
The destruction of Bhishma."

Scene Six

(Nine days of the great war have elapsed. The Pandavas are battered and broken. As a last resort, they approach the commander-in-chief of the opposing army seeking a resolution.)

BHISHMA:

The best of the warriors in my tent,
enemies we are by day,
but at dusk you are all my grandchildren.
Nine days have we fought.
I have unleashed terror, I know,
I have your morale destroyed.
But, you are my grandchildren,
even if we fight this war on opposing fronts;
you are the inheritors of my clan.

So, with love and joyous tears,
welcome to my abode!
What may I accomplish for you, my children?
I shall do it with all my soul.
You want the means of my death?
Counsel to defeat me? Your enemy?
Yes, you cannot acquire your kingdom
unless you have conquered me.
This destruction of warriors needs to be arrested.
I too am tired.
If knowing the means of my destruction
would help you end or win this war,
then so be it.
None of you are competent
to withstand me in battle.
I have no weakness, you see.
But you seek my death
to save yourselves from destruction,
to obtain victory.
And by God, you deserve it.
For all these years of travesty,
as long as I am alive, you cannot win.
You know this already, don't you?
When I fall, you will win.
Kill me without delay,
and you will have your victory, my sons.
Why these long faces?
I permit you to strike me.
When I am slaughtered,
all else will be slaughtered.

But know this:
I am incapable of being killed
by any warrior on your side.
There is none to best me, test me.
But if I were to be divested of my arms and weapons,
then yes, anyone can kill me at their pleasure.
Here is the secret, for you all seem bewildered,
of how to achieve this gentle task.
I don't like to fight a woman.
In fact, I won't.
I won't fight anyone
who bears a female appearance.
Call it my arrogance, but
I never fight the disabled,
and I don't fight mean men.
So, find someone in your army
who has one of the above traits
to challenge me.

You do have Shikhandi,
that first-born of Drupada.
Born a girl, that wrathful, valiant soldier.
Let her face me in battle.
Then, I won't fight.
Then, it will be easy for you to kill me… at least fell me.
I see a man who was once a woman as inauspicious.
Place this person in front and win.
Shikhandi has been born to bear my death, so I hear.
Rest well tonight;
tomorrow is your day.

Shikhandi, whether she strikes me or not,
I will never fight with her.
She is the same Shikhandi
the creator made a woman,
and will remain for me the same.
Go now and sleep,
the world knows:
I will never fight Shikhandi.

Scene Seven

(*Bhishma lies fallen on the battlefield. Shikhandi comes to meet Bhishma.*)

Shikhandi:

Bhishma, I salute you!
I heard you say,
"These are not Shikhandi's arrows,
they are Arjuna's for they tear my flesh
like the young of a crab rents its mother's body."
You did not want me to get
any acknowledgement for your fall.
I am not complaining.
I have killed ample men in the last ten days.
I asked Krishna to give you my message.

He refused, saying his mission was diplomatic
and he wouldn't carry personal missives.

Nothing much.
I wanted to let you know
when I endeavoured to return
the medicine man's penis,
it refused to go.
It stayed stuck to my body.

I went to the forest and met him
but he was living joyously as a woman,
and said he had no need for the appendage,
until the day of my death.
I wanted you to know I am a man
and that I challenged you to a single duel
on the very first day.
But my message never got delivered,
and you stuck to your arrogance,
turning your chariot away from me.

You will die when you decide to,
won't you, obstinate man?
The destruction of Bhishma is attained.
But the cost has run into severe
arrears of ages and ages.
So many that they are but a blur.
Only enchanting fires exist,
into which I had thrown myself,
again, and again,

to get closer to you.
Why? I don't know.
Love is no different from hate, is it?
The tenacious resolve, that perverse obstinacy.
I wanted to talk to you, Bhishma.
The last time we met,
you did not give me much opportunity to speak.
I saw that in a dream.
I, running inside a forest and
you, mocking me from a mound of skulls.
As I came closer, I saw all those skulls
belonged to me.

You hate Shikhandi.
I am an aberration to you.
The conduit of memories
freshened up and flowed
when I was revealed as a man
tormented by dreams,
tumultuous frenzies of yesteryears caught up.
Amba…
it's the name I heard in my dreams,
the name of a woman.
Gaunt, bronzed, a mad woman called Amba.
I sensed the desire of so many births
being finally fulfilled.
My body always smelt of smoke, tinder and fire.
Today, they are all subdued.
Your fall has achieved that, Bhishma.
The devils of my mind are curtailed.

I have burned a million times to reach you.
Bhishma, you were a conundrum
I was attempting to resolve for ages.
I was born with anger against you.
When you refused to include me in your list of warriors,
I was bemused.
Why, Bhishma?
For I was not born a man?
What is it to be born a man?
Born with an organ for planting seeds?
That's what a farmer does.
Why does a warrior need it?
You were born a man… with the manhood of a man.
How did it serve you, Bhishma?
Or how did you serve it?
What's the difference then between you and me,
if that's what being a man is?

I had a revelation, an epiphany, of revenge,
of malcontent and blood.
You chose to hide
your brother's incompetence in bed
by kidnapping women for him.
Killed men.
See what it did to your family?
It caused confusion.
Blind men, blinded women,
impotent men, barren women.
Now, your actions have caused this war.
See, Bhishma, aeons ago I demanded your destruction.

Birth after birth it multiplied.
And now your entire family,
my entire family will die.
You found my anger childish,
a scrawl on your egotistical tapestry.
The rent was tiny, but it grew.
It enlarged, it encompassed.
And now, the void is so huge
that everything belongs within it.
I don't know what I want anymore.
But I will participate and fight,
till this chapter is closed.

No more births, Bhishma.
I am done.
I have burned enough.
I don't forgive you.
Once again, you insulted me
by not fighting with me.
I will see you once all this is over.
I will come once more
to punish you, to remind you—
Shikhandi is a man.
Amba was a woman.
And you respected neither.
Goodbye.

THE END

Acknowledgements

My salutations to the writers, story-tellers and playwrights whose works have inspired me all my life to explore the squillion aspects of *The Mahabharata* again and again. I would like to express my gratitude to the prodigious translations of the epic by Kisari Mohan Ganguli, M N Dutt and Bibek Debroy.

V Balakrishnan is an actor, playwright, designer and an ICCR empaneled director. An alumnus of the Shri Ram Centre for Performing Arts and the National School of Drama, New Delhi, he is a Charles Wallace Scholar and a recipient of the Fulbright Distinguished Award in Teaching. Balakrishnan is the founder and artistic director of Theatre Nisha, Chennai, and has over 200 productions to his credit. His play *Sordid* won The Hindu Playwright Award 2019.

www.ingramcontent.com/pod-product-compliance
Lightning Source LLC
LaVergne TN
LVHW040323200726
843493LV00015B/2729